ONE DA

Meditations and Prayers on the Eleventh Step

A Message of Hope

Msgr. Joseph E. Farrell

LIGUORI
PUBLICATIONS

One Liguori Drive
Liguori, Missouri 63057
(314) 464-2500

Imprimi Potest:
Edmund T. Langton, C.SS.R.
Provincial, St. Louis Province
Redemptorist Fathers

Imprimatur:
+ Charles R. Koester
Vicar General, Archdiocese of St. Louis

ISBN 0-89243-056-7

Table of Contents

FOREWORD

Before the merciful change in legislation in many States, one of God's creatures often stood before a bar of justice on a charge of drunkenness! Wearied by a series of cases of like nature, the judge, knowing of no other recourse, rapped his gavel and said tersely: "Thirty days!" The sentence was imposed by society, and law and order demanded the payment of this debt. Although "thirty days" meant balancing the debit side of the ledger, it was also intended as an opportunity for the offender to realize and amend his fault. Statistics prove, however, that this was not the case. Too often, the prisoner returned to his old habits, more embittered against society and his fellow-man.

Thirty days in jail was imposed by society. This little booklet speaks of another thirty days cheerfully accepted by the individual who has achieved sobriety or is seeking sobriety through the Twelve Steps of Alcoholics Anonymous. The eleventh step of AA reads: "We sought through prayer and meditation to improve our conscious contact with God as we understood him, praying only for the knowledge of his will for us and the power to carry that out." Thirty days of prayer in gratitude to a Higher Power for sobriety is far more salutary than thirty days of punishment for offenses against temperance.

This booklet is intended for those who have attained sobriety through AA; however it may also be used by one who is seeking release from the alcoholic devil or monkey on his back. There are two ways of achieving sobriety. One is easy; the other is difficult. The easy way is through the fellowship and program of AA. The other is through sheer guts. If the reader is seeking release from alcoholic intemperance, we strongly recommend that he pick up the telephone book and call the local chapter of AA. If the local unit is on the ball (and it usually is), the AA will take over and lead you by the hand over the rough pathway each member traveled to achieve sobriety.

With this booklet in your hand, and in the quiet and peace of God's presence, read a chapter each day and then turn to the front of the booklet and read the designated prayers.

The AA member will begin this thirty days of prayer on the anniversary of his sobriety. You may also choose the month of your anniversary and begin on the first day of that month — this will make for easier counting.

Should this little booklet help you in any way, the author will consider himself amply repaid. Should you fulfill your debt of gratitude to a Higher Power through these days of prayer and meditation, then carry your gratitude and zeal into twelfth-step work "Having had a spiritual awakening as a result of these steps, we tried to carry this message to alcoholics and to practice these principles in all our affairs."

While this booklet is for those with an alcoholic problem, it can also benefit those with other problems in life. Take the AA way of living and apply it to your own life.

This booklet is best read the AA way — one day at a time.

PRAYERS TO BE SAID
DAILY AT THE
CONCLUSION OF MEDITATION

GOD LOVES ME — GOD WILL HELP ME

Let me realize that easy does it . . .

Our Father, who art in heaven, hallowed be thy name; thy kingdom come; thy will be done on earth as it is in heaven. Give us this day our daily bread, and forgive us our trespasses, as we forgive those who trespass against us; and lead us not into temptation but deliver us from evil. For thine is the kingdom, and the power, and the glory for ever and ever. Amen.

Teach me how to live my life one day at a time . . .

God, grant me the serenity
To accept the things I cannot change,
Courage to change the things I can,
And wisdom to know the difference.

Show me how to put first things first . . .

Lord, make me an instrument of your peace.
Where there is hatred, let me sow love;
Where there is injury, pardon;
Where there is doubt, faith;
Where there is despair, hope;
Where there is darkness, light;
Where there is sadness, joy.
O divine Master, grant that I may seek not so much
To be consoled as to console;

To be understood as to understand;
To be loved as to love;
For it is in giving that we receive;
It is in pardoning that we are pardoned;
And it is in dying that we are born to eternal life. Amen.

By the grace of God, I can master it . . .

Thank you, heavenly Father, for all the yesterdays
and all the yesteryears.
Thank you for the new day in my life.
Help me to live it the very best way possible
and to be worthy of your love.

THE TWELVE STEPS

We
1. Admitted we were powerless over alcohol . . . that our lives had become unmanageable.
2. Came to believe that a Power greater than ourselves could restore us to sanity.
3. Made a decision to turn our will and our lives over to the care of God as we understood him.
4. Made a searching and fearless moral inventory of ourselves.
5. Admitted to God, to ourselves, and to another human being the exact nature of our wrongs.
6. Were entirely ready to have God remove all these defects of character.
7. Humbly asked him to remove our shortcomings.
8. Made a list of all persons we had harmed and became willing to make amends to them all.
9. Made direct amends to such people wherever possible, except when to do so would injure them or others.
10. Continued to take personal inventory and when we were wrong promptly admitted it.
11. Sought through prayer and meditation to improve our conscious contact with God as we understood him, praying only for knowledge of his will for us and the power to carry that out.
12. Tried to carry this message to alcoholics and to practice these principles in all our affairs.

1

FAITH

Back in the days of sailing vessels, a young and inexperienced seaman was sent aloft in a storm to disentangle the snarled ropes of the mainmast. He accomplished the ascent with the quickness of the young. Nevertheless, the descent frightened him as he gazed down at the tossing ship so far below him. The lurching deck rocking in the wind and storm froze him to the mainmast. All he could see was the fury of the storm in the tossing of the boat and the force of the wind. The captain below, sensing his danger, shouted: "Don't look down, son, look up!" The boy looked above him. The heavens were stable and quiet and immovable. By looking up to God in his heaven, the boy forgot the fury of the storm and the tossing of the boat and easily made his descent to the safety of the deck.

The alcoholic who has attained sobriety has weathered the greatest storm of his life. Yet, the winds of compulsion do not cease to blow because he has weathered a major storm. There will be other big storms in his life. It is this failure to realize that other storms will arise that account for the slips of the alcoholic. He must realize that he will be an alcoholic until he dies. The progress of alcoholism continues despite months and years of sobriety. Lack of belief in this truth will result in slipping back or, at least, rough going in the future.

It is better to admit that you are powerless over alcohol. Constant repetition of this fact, one day at a time, will build a wall that the alcoholic devil cannot surmount. Wouldn't it be grand if there were no more storms in your life? However, this is not so, for the very storms that blew during the days of wine and roses will continue to buffet you in the years ahead. When the winds blow, look up to God and be neither terrified nor hurt by the storms of compulsion and temptation.

It is wise to fortify our homes during a hurricane, but it is far better to observe hurricane warnings and to put the safety rules into effect before the storm strikes. The alcoholic knows the danger signals. When they appear, seek out God or a fellow AA member, as the storm is about to break.

You must first believe that God can help you. You must then believe that God will help you. It is this belief in a Higher Power that is the cornerstone of AA.

In the succeeding chapters of this booklet we hope to be able to bring you to a realization that God does love you personally and individually. If a sparrow does not fall to the ground but that God sees it, how much more does he care for you for whom he died on the Cross. God loves you and will help you, but you must turn to him through prayer and meditation.

There was a rugged individual in the New Testament by the name of Paul. He was buffeted by storms and dashed about by shipwreck, yet was able to say: "There is nothing I cannot master with the help of the one who gives me strength" (Phil 4:13).

2

_____ **SECOND DAY**

GRATITUDE

"As he entered one of the villages, ten lepers came to meet him. They stood some way off and called to him, 'Jesus, Master, take pity on us.' When he saw them, he said: 'Go and show yourselves to the priests.' Now as they were going away they were cleansed. Finding himself cured, one of them turned back praising God at the top of his voice and threw himself at the feet of Jesus and thanked him. The man was a Samaritan. This made Jesus say, 'Were not all ten made clean? The other nine, where are they? It seems that no one has come back to give praise to God except this foreigner.' He said to the man, 'Stand up and go on your way. Your faith has saved you' "(Lk 17:12-19).

We wonder if the founders of AA had this story from the Gospel in mind when they wrote the eleventh step. Possibly not, but they did realize in writing the fundamental principles of AA that it is important that we be grateful to almighty God for the gift of sobriety.

Let us meditate on this story. Leprosy was a misunderstood disease in the days of Christ. A leper was an outcast of society. He could not live in his own home. He had to make the best of things outside the town apart from his fellow-man lest he contaminate him. More than that, he had to carry a bell with him, and whenever anyone approached, he was obliged by law to cry out, "Unclean, unclean." His friends and others were warned to keep away from him. When the ten lepers approached our Lord, they believed that he could help them. They neglected the cry of the unclean, sensing that it made no difference to him. Society was not interested nor did it understand their problems, but they felt that this Healer took compassion on them and would restore them to sanity of body.

Is it far-fetched to compare the alcoholic to the leper? Science has made rapid strides in the treatment of leprosy because this disease is now understood. There is even talk of eliminating the isolation technique in the treatment of leprosy.

The leper obtains help today because medical science understands his case. So, too, the alcoholic receives aid when he is understood or, better yet, when he understands himself.

Others may sense that a man is an alcoholic, but only the afflicted individual can and must help himself by admitting that he is an alcoholic.

"A leper came to him and pleaded on his knees: 'If you want to,' he said, 'you can cure me.' Feeling sorry for him, Jesus stretched out his hand and touched him. 'Of course I want to!' he said. 'Be cured!' (Mk 1:40-41) The first step of AA is admission, the second is belief, and the third is decision. If the alcoholic can follow these three primary steps, he is well on the road to sobriety.

There are ten commandments of God and not nine. There are twelve steps of AA and not only three. We can get by with three steps but if we wish to fulfill the program, we must strive to follow the twelve steps. The eleventh step must not be neglected. As you pray this day, you are fulfilling the eleventh step by seeking to improve your conscious contact with God.

A cynic once said: "For gratitude give me dogs." Never let it be said that the alcoholic, like the nine lepers in the Gospel, is failing in his debt of gratitude to the Higher Power.

_____ **THIRD DAY**

REWARDS

"Then it was Peter's turn to say to him: 'Here we have put everything aside to follow you. What can we expect from it?' Jesus said to them, 'I give you my solemn word, in the new age when the Son of Man takes his seat upon a throne befitting his glory, you who have followed me shall likewise take your places on twelve thrones to judge the twelve tribes of Israel' " (Mt 19:27-28).

Peter is very likeable. He is also very human. His human weaknesses and his inherent strength and goodness make a great deal of sense to the alcoholic. We shall speak of him often in these pages as we think over his attitude in the above Gospel incident.

Peter was bragging. He made a great deal of all the things that he had left. Peter was a fisherman and a poor man. What did he leave behind? A few fishing nets and a boat were the sum of his earthly possessions. He looked for a reward for what he had left behind, not realizing that his reward was in the new life of the apostolate that he was assuming. Christ spoke tenderly to him and promised him a heavenly reward.

What does the alcoholic leave behind? He leaves the consolation of the jug that was killing him slowly. Big deal! The diabetic leaves behind his God-given taste for sweets. The ulcer patient leaves behind his taste for fried foods. Big deal! When we receive more in return than what we sacrifice, the result can be measured only in terms of a big deal.

The alcoholic can right now dwell briefly on some of the sad days he has left behind; the possibility of a wet brain, the incidence of an enlarged liver, unhappy relatives, irrevocable words and actions uttered and performed under the influence of alcohol. Better left behind than cultivated!

Peter left behind so little and gained so much in the new life that was afforded to him. If the alcoholic will be grateful to the Higher Power for the gift of sobriety, then he will have no room in his thinking for regrets in leaving behind the days of wine and roses, the days of jumpy nerves and upset stomachs, the days of bitterness and remorse, the days of resentment and self-pity.

Sobriety is its own reward. No regrets are in order. Yet, it is consoling to know that the blood and sweat and tears that have been shed are not unnoticed by the Higher Power. The same God who promised a heavenly reward to Peter is aware of the sacrifices, struggles, and victories that go into the making of a new man. God loves me! God knows what I suffer! God will help me! God will reward me!

PRAYER

Our Father, who art in heaven, hallowed be thy name; thy kingdom come; thy will be done on earth as it is in heaven. Give us this day our daily bread, and forgive us our debts as we forgive our debtors; and lead us not into temptation but deliver us from evil. Amen. *(Revised Standard Version)*

It is amazing the progress that science has made in the field of medicine. Tuberculosis has been practically eliminated. In Connecticut, buildings formerly used for the treatment of tuberculosis have been turned into institutions for care of long-term patients. Diabetes has insulin as its control. Cardiac ailments, long a number-one killer, are diagnosed and treated with far-reaching results for the patients' welfare.

In the field of alcoholism, success has not been startling in the world of medicine. Alcoholics Anonymous has achieved outstanding results in the recovery of the alcoholic. This organization is not the result of medical science — its success may be called a spiritual phenomenon.

If God loves alcoholics, and he does, then it is not wishful thinking to believe that he wants them to obtain the necessary help through a beneficial program. With a tip of the hat to medical science, we firmly believe that AA has the answers and is a giant step in the recovery of alcoholics.

So it is that the *Lord's Prayer* is the inspired prayer of AA. The apostles said simply: "Lord, teach us to pray." Our Lord answered, "So you should pray like this: 'Our Father in heaven . . .' " (Mt 6:9-13). The good Lord wishes us to pray to a Higher Power. He taught us the above prayer for this purpose. It is difficult to go wrong when we use it.

'Give us this day, our daily bread.' We are asking the Higher Power for what we need whether of body or soul. It is a prayer that is geared to daily recitation. Do you say it every day? How much it reminds us of "One day at a time."

'And forgive us our debts.' We project this into the eighth and ninth steps. We cannot close our eyes completely to the facts that we have incurred debts and stepped on many toes in the days when we were bouncing high, wide, and handsome.

'As we forgive our debtors.' Resentment is a serious fault in the usual alcoholic. It isn't easy to rid oneself of this vice. Yet, unless we do, the ugly serpent of resentment is apt to rear its head, and brother, if it does, the ensuing slip can be as harmful as the poison of a cobra. Really mean it when you recite the *Lord's Prayer*. Don't let resentment ruin the sobriety you have attained.

'And lead us not into temptation.' Your alcoholic weakness will be with you until you die. Face it. One day at a time. It should be consoling to know that you are asking for grace and strength to get through each day without a bounce or a slip.

'But deliver us from evil.' We need the help of the Higher Power to see us through each day. The cocktail hour, the sociable drink, the cooling pause that refreshes, the lift of a boilermaker, the euphoria, etc., will always surround you. But through AA you are made strong. Evil will seek you out. Don't go looking for it.

LOVING FORGIVENESS

St. Luke records the following parable told by Jesus: ''A man had two sons. The younger said to his father, 'Father, let me have the share of the estate that would come to me.' So the father divided the property between them. A few days later, the younger son got together everything he had and left for a distant country where he squandered his money on a life of debauchery.

''When he had spent it all, that country experienced a severe famine, and now he began to feel the pinch, so he hired himself out to one of the local inhabitants who put him on his farm to feed the pigs. And he would willingly have filled his belly with the husks the pigs were eating but no one offered him anything. Then he came to his senses and said, 'How many of my father's paid servants have more food than they want, and here am I dying of hunger! I will leave this place and go to my father and say: Father, I have sinned against heaven and against you; I no longer deserve to be called your son; treat me as one of your paid servants.' So he left the place and went back to his father.

''While he was still a long way off, his father saw him and was moved with pity. He ran to the boy, clasped him in his arms and kissed him tenderly. Then his son said, 'Father, I have sinned against heaven and against you. I no longer deserve to be called your son.' But the father said to his servants, 'Quick! Bring out the best robe and put it on him; put a ring on his finger and sandals on his feet. Bring the calf we have been fattening, and kill it; we are going to have a feast, a celebration, because this son of mine was dead and has come back to life; he was lost and is found' '' (Lk 15:11-24).

History doesn't tell us whether the prodigal son was an alcoholic or not. He could have been, although the incidence of alcoholism in the Semites is very low. We do know that our Lord told this parable to point out the love of God for the sinner. With God, the sinner can return to his Father's home if he recognizes his sin and is sorry for it.

The prodigal fulfilled the first three steps of AA. He recognized his fault. He believed that his father would help him. He made the decision to throw himself on the mercy of his father.

The outstanding feature of this parable is the fact that the prodigal knows where his home is and feels the surety of care and protection there and only there. AA is the home of the alcoholic. If he recognizes this and hurries to his home, he will be safe. Especially in the matter of slips and bounces, the alcoholic should know where home is. If he slips, then he must get back home as quickly as possible. The AA meeting is home. Saturation in AA reading is home. Christian charity in twelfth-step work is home.

When the prodigal returned home, he would have been satisfied to become a servant, but the father of the home was most generous. He prepared a feast for the return of the son who was lost. Through the grace of almighty God, the alcoholic is restored to his original status of dignity. What a joy to meet one who has sobriety! Notice how he holds his head high, his shoulders back, and how he impresses the onlooker with his strength and manliness.

Home is the hunter, home from the hill. Home is the sailor, home from the sea. Home is the alcoholic, home from the "far country" where his fair-weather friends deserted him.

ALTRUISM

Jesus one day told the following parable: ''. . . A man was once on his way down from Jerusalem to Jericho and fell into the hands of brigands; they took all he had, beat him and then made off, leaving him half-dead. Now a priest happened to be traveling down the same road, but when he saw the man, he passed by on the other side. In the same way a Levite who came to the place saw him, and passed by on the other side. But a Samaritan traveler who came upon him was moved with compassion when he saw him. He went up and bandaged his wounds, pouring oil and wine on them. He then lifted him on to his own mount, carried him to the inn and looked after him. Next day, he took out two denarii and handed them to the innkeeper. 'Look after him,' he said, 'and on my way back I will make good any extra expense you have' '' (Lk 10:30-35).

The parable of the Good Samaritan is the twelfth step in action. We must not judge the priest and the Levite too harshly. They did not know what to do. In our resentment, we are apt to judge harshly those who could have helped and did not and those who made it possible for us to continue in our drinking. Resentful judgments have no place in the rehabilitation of the alcoholic.

Many alcoholics have outstanding success in twelfth-step work. Others do not do so well. Some men are born salesmen. Some are extroverts in that they like to talk to people. Remember to do your twelfth-step work and if you are not equipped to talk and to sell, you can at least pray.

Kneel or sit in the quiet of your room and pray and meditate. Do it every day, one day at a time. Mention in prayer the names of those you know who have a monkey on their backs. The poet says that more things are wrought by prayer than this world dreams of. Some are brought to sobriety by talking and selling. God alone knows how many have returned home through the power of prayer.

There is also the power of fellowship. Some are immune to any amount of talking and selling, but there usually is a crack in their armor through which acts of patience, kindness, and fellowship can penetrate. This is the area in which the quiet alcoholic can help the drinker. Merely state: "I am an alcoholic; I would like to be your friend." It can work where talking and selling have been known to fail.

In the parable, the Good Samaritan promised to look in upon his return. Please don't be discouraged if one of the newcomers bounces. Please don't give up on him. Prayer and love can bring him back to sobriety.

The Samaritans did not enjoy a good reputation among the Jews who looked down on them. It is noteworthy that our Lord overlooked the faults of the Samaritan and paid tribute to his inherent goodness. An alcoholic does not enjoy a good reputation with his associates who knew him during his drinking days. How consoling it is that the good Lord overlooks the glaring faults and recognizes the goodness that lies beneath. Never sell a man short. Even the most evil can gain greatness. A man named Augustine is proof of that. Never write off a compulsive drinker no matter how low he has sunk. AA has thousands in its ranks.

7
_____ SEVENTH DAY

PERSEVERANCE

There was a man by the name of Augustine. He really sowed wild oats in his youth. His mother, Monica, never ceased to pray for his conversion. It is said that one day he heard a voice which said to him:

"Take and read." He chose a copy of the Bible and the first verse that struck his eye was, "Let your armour be the Lord Jesus Christ; forget about satisfying your bodies with all their cravings" (Rom 13:13-14). The grace of God touched his heart and his conversion made a saint of a sinner.

This is one of many examples in religious history that runs parallel to the story of an alcoholic. In the history of alcoholism, there are some who maintained that the "light" of God's grace made a vivid impression in their lives. It is not necessary to have a seemingly visible manifestation of God's grace in the life of the alcoholic; it is sufficient that he correspond to the grace of the Higher Power in whatsoever manner it comes to him.

There is a value in persevering prayer for the dissolute. Monica never ceased to pray for her son Augustine. What is worthwhile gaining is worthwhile waiting for and praying for with unfailing perseverance. Have you ever prayed for a newcomer and then became discouraged? Suppose the one who prayed for you had let you down?

The grace of God came to Augustine through reading. Many an alcoholic gets jumpy when he leaves the protection of his weekly meeting to take his family on vacation. AA meetings are held all over the world, but it is possible that one will not always be conveniently held. This is where reading comes in handy. Some travelers will bring a Bible with them. The Bible for the alcoholic is the Big Book. There are many other books which he can read. Reading is not a substitute for the meeting, but it will help to offset complacency that arises when absent from the influence of AA fellowship.

Americans are deluged by magazines of all descriptions. Subscribers to our national magazines run into the millions. Each one has his favorite. The "must" for the alcoholic is the AA Grapevine. This may be obtained from The Alcoholics Anonymous Grapevine, Inc., 468 Park Avenue, South, New York, New York 10016. Be a reader and a booster for AA Grapevine. There are many worthwhile articles pertinent to your needs in each issue. However, it must not be used as a substitute for the meeting.

In the February 1964 issue of AA Grapevine, there is an excellent article entitled "Abraham Lincoln on Alcoholism." Lincoln showed a profound insight into the problem of the habitual drunkard. This address was delivered in 1842 to a temperance society and Abe Lincoln proved that he was a hundred years ahead of time in his thinking.

The following quotation will perk us up a bit: "Indeed, I believe if we take habitual drunkards as a class, their heads and their hearts will bear an advantageous comparison with those of any other class." Also, "Those who have suffered by intemperance and have reformed are the most powerful and efficient instruments to push the reformation to ultimate success." Again, "If you would win a man to your cause, first convince him that you are his sincere friend."

"Take up and read." We are proud of Lincoln for being so far ahead of his time. A tip of the hat to the AA Grapevine for its monthly analysis of alcoholism.

--- **EIGHTH DAY**

CONFRONTATION

Jesus, speaking of the Second Coming, one day told his disciples: "It will be the same as it was in Lot's day: people were eating and drinking, buying and selling, planting and building, but the day Lot left Sodom, God rained fire and brimstone from heaven and it destroyed them all. It will be the same when the day comes for the Son of Man to be revealed. When that day comes, anyone on the housetop, with his possessions in the house, must not come down to collect them, nor must anyone in the fields turn back either. Remember Lot's wife" (Lk 17:28-32).

You may read in the Book of Genesis, chapter nineteen, the story of Lot and his wife. They were told to flee from Sodom before it was destroyed and were commanded not to look back on the unfortunate city. Lot's wife disobeyed and was turned into a pillar of salt.

Likewise, the alcoholic must never look back upon his drinking days with fondness in his eyes. It is certain that he will not be turned into a pillar of salt, but he can be hurt in a far worse way by losing his hard-won sobriety.

There is a way, however, in which the alcoholic can look back. In fact, he is instructed by the twelve steps to do just that. It is a bit sad that the alcoholic is content often with recognition, belief, and decision (the first three steps) and forgets to go on with the other nine. The fourth, fifth, eighth, and ninth, and tenth specifically instruct him to look back on the misspent days of his life.

The fourth step reads: "We made a searching and fearless moral inventory of ourselves." The fifth step: "We admitted to God, to ourselves, and to another human being the exact nature of our wrongs." The eighth step: "We made a list of all persons we had harmed and became willing to make amends to them all." The ninth step: "We made direct amends to such people wherever possible, except when to do so would injure them or others." The tenth step: "We continued to take a personal inventory and when we were wrong, promptly admitted it."

In the fifth step, tell your inventory to another trustworthy person — one who can keep your secrets — a trusted friend. He need not be a member of AA or an alcoholic — just someone who is willing to listen to you and your troubles.

In the fifth step, the alcoholic takes on the role of a prosecuting attorney rather than the defense attorney. It is so easy to justify our past actions, but unfortunately it does not help much in maintaining sobriety. Prosecute your case history with the intensity of a district attorney.

We think of restitution in terms of money. At times, it is easy to restore money and to pay our bad bills. It is not as easy to make up to people for the harm and the hurt caused them.

The eighth step advises that you make a list of those you have harmed and the ninth step directs that you make amends wherever it is possible. It takes a lot of courage. Sobriety is not an easy matter. It is like a boy sliding downhill on a sled. He whizzes down the hill. Not so easy coming back! However, it is important to fulfill all the steps of

AA. There are some who can get by on just three: recognition, belief, and decision. But if they think these three steps are sufficient for them, they are mistaken.

9

HUMILITY

There is a story of a man who lived in a soldier's home and gained a reputation for his sanctity. A newspaper reporter wished to write a story about this man and rang the bell of the home. He inquired: "I am looking for the man in this home who is known for his sanctity." The man who opened the door bowed his head, lowered his eyelids, and answered: "I am he." He thereby added another feather to his cap but lost the headlines of a story.

So many men in AA claim that it is difficult to get a good definition of humility. The man who says, "I have achieved sobriety and am proud of it," may be headed for a bounce. The twelve steps of AA are saturated with the virtue of humility. If you follow the twelve steps faithfully, you won't need a definition of humility. However, humility may be described as "a recognition of the truth." A great spiritual writer once wrote: "I'd rather have humility than be able to define it."

If a man is a compulsive drinker, then no amount of pious pratings will change him one iota. It is when he comes to recognize for himself his drinking problem that he begins the ascent to sobriety. The first step is loaded with humility.

While humility permeates the whole twelve steps, we single out the seventh and the tenth for special attention. The seventh step is: "We humbly asked him to remove our shortcomings." If we admit that we are powerless over alcohol and if we depend on the Higher Power for help, we are really practicing humility. God's grace, like his sunshine and fresh air, is so much a part of our lives that we take it for granted. If we assume to ourselves the credit for our sobriety, then we are failing in humility. We recognize the truth that it is by the grace of God that we are sober.

The tenth step is: "We continued to take personal inventory and, when we were wrong, promptly admitted it." AA does more than make a man sober — it makes him more of a man. It takes a real man to admit that he is wrong. It takes a still greater man to take inventory of his daily life in order to make amends.

The Greek philosophers taught: "Know thyself." The tenth step helps the alcoholic to know himself. It was humility that gained sobriety for him, and it will be humility that will win character. How sad it is for an alcoholic to be self-satisfied with sobriety and to have no further interest in building his character!

The Matt Talbot Retreat League publishes a small card: "The man in the glass." If the alcoholic can look at himself in the mirror and honestly admit that he has faults, he is practicing the virtue of humility. He may be able to deceive others, but he can never deceive himself for very long.

Humility is the recognition of truth. Recognition is the first step, and it is humility. Belief is the second step, and it is humility. Decision is the third step, and it is humility. The seventh and tenth steps are saturated with the virtue of humility. The twelve steps are truth. The twelve steps are humility. When one accepts three steps and disregards the other nine, then he is failing in truth.

TRUST

The story is told of a famous opera singer who loved her father very much. Each week she sent him a very generous check for his own use. From time to time he would write to her and ask for money over and above the weekly allotment. She graciously answered these requests because of her great love for her father. The demands, however, became increasingly heavier and she began to be irritated and annoyed. Still she sent the extra checks to her father. When the stock market crashed in 1929, she was impoverished and became a poor woman overnight. Then her father came to her with a bank book in which every check had been deposited in her name.

The Higher Power deals in like fashion with the alcoholic. He makes many demands which may easily be a cause of irritation and annoyance. Through these meditations and prayers on the eleventh step, the alcoholic can increase his faith to such a high degree that his trust in his Father will offset any irritations which may arise.

Our Lord said on one occasion: "Do not store up treasures for yourselves on earth, where moths and woodworms destroy them and thieves can break in and steal. But store up treasures for yourselves in heaven, where neither moth nor woodworms destroy them and thieves cannot break in and steal. For where your treasure is, there will your heart be also" (Mt 6:19-21).

Our lives are so closely bound up in the rigors of daily living that we lose sight of the love of our heavenly Father.

On another occasion Jesus said: "If any man will come after me, let him take up his cross daily and follow me" (Lk 9:23). An alcoholic disease is a cross of monumental proportion; however, the daily crosses that the alcoholic carries are very important in the formation of his character.

This may be difficult to believe, but it is often easier to make a supreme sacrifice or to perform a heroic act than to suffer and overcome the daily annoyances. In building character, it is more difficult to perform the actions of the day with patience than it is to make the decision to turn our lives over to the care of a Higher Power.

If the alcoholic can take up his cross daily, he is in reality following after our Lord. "Easy does it." One day at a time. What a familiar ring this has. How beautifully do the teachings of the Gospel blend into the daily life of the alcoholic.

"Jesus went about doing good" (Acts 10:38). He was kind, considerate, and merciful. When you add these to the character of the alcoholic, he really is fulfilling the twelve steps.

Kindness, consideration, and mercy are virtues implicitly contained in the twelve steps. AA is both a selfish and an unselfish program. Charity is the greatest of the virtues. The AA member does not preach charity as such, but each step he takes in the daily routine of the twelfth step is charity in action.

POWERLESSNESS

Remember the Gospel story of the blind man from Jericho? "Now as he drew near to Jericho there was a blind man sitting at the side of the road begging. When he heard the crowd going past he asked what it was all about, and they told him that Jesus the Nazarene was passing by. So he called out, 'Jesus, Son of David, have pity on me.' The people in front scolded him and told him to keep quiet, but he shouted all the louder, 'Son of David, have pity on me.' Jesus stopped and ordered them to bring the man to him, and when he came up, asked him, 'What do you want me to do for you?' 'Sir,' he replied, 'let me see again.' Jesus said to him, 'Receive your sight. Your faith has saved you.' And instantly his sight returned and he followed him praising God, and all the people who saw it gave praise to God for what had happened'' (Lk 18:35-43).

The blind man was sure of one thing in his heart. He knew that Jesus could help him. This is the key to sobriety for the alcoholic. It is the second step: "We came to believe that a Power greater than ourselves could restore us to sanity." In AA, sobriety gives sight to a man blinded by alcoholism. If he slips or bounces, he may easily lose his sight again. Faith through the second step can again restore his sight.

The blind man cried out: "Jesus, Son of David, have mercy on me." How often have we heard: "Can't somebody help me?" Yes, there is somebody who is willing and who can aid you. It is your local chapter of AA. How sad it was before AA came into being! No one seemed to touch the core of the alcoholic's need. Doctors, psychiatrists, and clergymen endeavored to do their best, but they did not have the secret formula of AA.

People standing around the blind man rebuked him. How many times have you personally been rebuked, scolded, derided, shouted at by those who do not know the help that is given by the Higher Power through the fellowship of AA.

Jesus commanded that the blind man be brought to him. This is the twelfth step of AA. God can deal directly with the afflicted. However, he often chooses to deal with the alcoholic through the instrumentality of other human beings. The Higher Power wills that you be his co-worker by bringing the man blinded by alcoholism to AA and to him.

The blind man knew that he was powerless to cure his own blindness. That is step one. He believed that Jesus could help him — step two. He cried out and turned to Jesus — step three. Immediately he regained his sight, and he returned thanks by following and glorifying Christ. Lest we forget — there are twelve steps and not only three. In the twelve steps, one must try to improve his conscious contact with God.

"And all the people who saw it gave praise to God." AA is a spiritual phenomenon. Society gives praise to AA for its great work. Humble doctors and psychiatrists must admit that AA has the answer which they have been searching for. Group therapy, self-expression, fellowship, or what have you — these are the ingredients. A tip of the hat to AA. An orchid to AA. We humbly give praise to God who works through AA.

AVAILABILITY

Here is another well-remembered story about our Lord: "Jesus entered Jericho and was going through the town when a man whose name was Zacchaeus made his appearance; he was one of the senior tax collectors and a wealthy man. He was anxious to see what kind of man Jesus was, but he was too short and could not see him for the crowd; so he ran ahead and climbed a sycamore tree to catch a glimpse of Jesus who was to pass that way. When Jesus reached the spot he looked up and spoke to him: 'Zacchaeus, come down. Hurry, because I must stay at your house today.' And he hurried down and welcomed him joyfully" (Lk 19:1-6).

We live in a hurry-up world. The man who is without a car is almost helpless. We miss so many people as we rush from one place to another. Our Lord walked the roads of Palestine, and he was always accessible to the people. The apostles tried to send away the crowds, but Christ would not allow it. It is a consolation to the alcoholic that the Higher Power is accessible to him and that he can turn to God with surety in all his problems.

If we wish to speak with the Pope or the President or the Governor, we need an appointment. The accessibility of our Lord! No appointment is needed. Just kneel or sit in the church of your home and he is present to you.

"And there was a man who came to him and asked, 'Good Master, what good deed must I do to possess eternal life?' Jesus said to him, 'Why do you ask me about what is good? There is one alone who is good. But if you wish to enter into life, keep the commandments' " (Mt 19:16-17). This young man received a direct answer from Christ. We do not enjoy this privilege of talking to our Lord face-to-face but if we really believe the second step of AA, we know that he does hear and that he will help us in our difficulties.

Perhaps you complain that you cannot hear the Lord. That is what you say. You did hear him when you put the third step into practice by making the most important decision of your life, the turning over of your will and your life to the care of God. In the quiet of prayer and meditation you can renew that step.

Zacchaeus approached the Lord and talked to him. Through this meditation and prayer, the eleventh step, you are drawing near to the Lord. Tell him what you need. Put the eighth step into practice. Pray for those you have hurt. You may not be able to define humility, but the eighth step is humility in action.

It is very good to talk. But don't talk too much. Try to listen to the Lord, and he will speak to your heart — speak to you about how you can improve your conscious contact with him as you understand him. An alcoholic who feels that he has made the supreme sacrifice, who feels that there is no room for improvement in his life, may be headed for trouble. Be humble. Be prayerful. Be the man the Lord intended you to be.

UNDERSTANDING

I like Zacchaeus. He was low in stature. He was just a small man. He had, however, virtues that the alcoholic needs. He was humble, just, and charitable. He was a rich man, but he was humble. He was willing to share his goods with others.

How the world regards the alcoholic! Like Zacchaeus, he is small in stature. Our Lord saw goodness in Zacchaeus, and he sees the good in the alcoholic. The following words of Abraham Lincoln reecho Christ's feeling for the alcoholic. "Indeed, I believe if we take habitual drunkards as a class, their heads and their hearts will bear an advantageous comparison with those of any other class."

Our Lord was born in a stable. He lived as a poor man. The foxes had dens, and the birds of the air had their nests; but the Son of Man had no place to rest his head. This should appeal to the boys on skid row. Our Lord died naked on the Cross. Does he understand the sickness and the misery and the remorse of the alcoholic? You know that he does.

Zacchaeus climbed a sycamore tree to see our Lord. There is effort expended in climbing a tree. The alcoholic must work hard to achieve his sobriety. Many times it takes sheer guts, but AA makes it possible.

Our Lord bade Zacchaeus to come down from the sycamore tree. He invited himself into his home. Realize that he invited himself in — he did not force himself upon Zacchaeus. The decision in the third step is the work of the individual. Others may help but the individual alone can make the decision. The Higher Power will help us, but he does not force himself upon us any more that we can force a drunkard to stop drinking.

Our Lord dined in the home of Zacchaeus. For the Matt Talbot-eer, this is a clear invitation to receive Holy Communion often. At the Last Supper our Lord shared the meal with his apostles when he changed bread and wine into his own Body and Blood. When the followers of Matt Talbot attend Holy Mass and receive Holy Communion, they are participating with our Lord and the apostles at the Last Supper.

Zacchaeus received our Lord with joy. What joy sobriety has brought to you! Sobriety is a part of real spirituality. Real spirituality brings joy with justice, charity, and kindness.

The same Christ who sought out Zacchaeus and the prodigal son and the lost sheep has a loving care for the alcoholic. He came to seek and save that which was lost. If you have been saved from the dizziness of the merry-go-round, then go out and seek to save others who have been lost. This you do through the twelfth step. That is real spirituality.

FOURTEENTH DAY

RENEWAL

Friends came to clean the desk of a Cardinal who had died. On the top of the desk, plainly in use, was the following prayer:

Tire not of new beginnings:
Build thy life, never on regret
Always upon resolve!
Shed no tear on the blotted page of the past,
But turn the leaf — and smile —
To see the clean white page before thee.

Tire not of new beginnings! The life of sobriety is a new beginning.

The Chinese have a proverb which says that before a man can complete a journey he must take the first step. At the first meeting of AA, a new beginning is made — the first step of a journey is taken. The journey will never be completed if you allow yourself to become tired and discouraged. We are impressed by the motto of the Salvation Army: "A man may be down, but he is never out." Each discouragement that is conquered gives strength to face the new problems that may arise in the journey on the road to sobriety.

Turn to prayer in time of discouragement. The eleventh step is not thrown in just to make twelve steps. It is there for a purpose. With spiritual insight, the founders of AA knew that discouragement would come, knew further that the strength to combat discouragement would come through prayer. In most cases prayer is ineffectual in conquering alcoholism. This may sound like heresy to the believer, but prayer with AA is much, much more effective than prayer without AA.

Build your life on the resolve to follow the AA program in its entirety. Many cities have been completely destroyed and then rebuilt by willing hands. The alcoholic has his rock bottom, be it high or low. By the time that bottom is reached, his life is usually a shambles. The twelve steps of AA are excellent for rebuilding the life of a drunkard. To make the building ready for occupancy, the first three steps are the foundation. The other nine are the maintenance steps and without constant attention to these, decay can set in. The Bible tells us that unless the Lord build the city, they labor in vain who build it — the eleventh step.

Build thy life, never on regret. No one will ever be able to understand the remorse of the drunkard but the alcoholic himself. Remorse fits into the picture when a man is drinking; but it has no place when he has earned sobriety. Dante says that there is no greater sorrow than to think of happy days in time of misery. This applies to the drinking man; it has no place in the thinking of the man who is sober. Regret would only glamorize the "kick" of drinking and would obscure the real miseries that were suffered at the time.

You didn't know that you were in the building business, did you? You are not building a house, but you are building a life. Check your foundation from time to time. Remember that constant maintenance makes for a good building.

15

RESOLUTIONS

To return to the Cardinal's prayer mentioned previously:
Build thy life, never on regret
Always upon resolve!
Shed no tear on the blotted page of the past,
But turn the leaf — and smile —
To see the clean white page before thee.

Build thy life . . . always upon resolve! Before the foundation of AA, it was common practice for a man to take a pledge. He would make a promise (resolve) to abstain from all alcoholic liquors. Some jokers would classify beer as nonliquor and then they would be off and running.

Then there were those who would abstain during Lent. To give credit where credit is due, many of them could do it. To compound problems, the bock would be running good before Lent was finished — and the resolve would be finished before Lent was finished. If you are compulsive, then do not make any comparisons with other drinkers for it will only lead to trouble — bad trouble.

The member of AA is building his life on resolve. What can be missed is the attention that should be given to steps four through twelve.

I have often told people that almighty God has a full and happy life ahead for them. It is theirs for the asking. Must it be done through blood and sweat and tears? What is worthwhile getting is worthwhile working for.

Shed no tear on the blotted page of the past. Cartoonists depict Ole Man Prohibition as a real sad sack. It would hurt him to smile. If one achieves sobriety, he is to be congratulated; but if he is continually shedding tears on what he has given up, oh brother! Remember the woman who never knew her husband drank until one day he came home sober. Never let it be said of you that you were easier to live with when drunk than when sober.

But turn the leaf — and smile — to see the clean white page before thee. You may have messed up your life in the past, but it doesn't do any good to dwell upon it. Your whole future is before you. What are you doing about it?

There are many clean pages before you in your life. They are to be filled by you. Live your life one day at a time. Keep the life clean generally and the old alcoholic devil will have less of a chance to overcome.

If you get a newcomer through the twelfth step and he makes good, you are to be congratulated. Don't rest on your laurels. Don't stop and say that your reputation is made and that you have paid your debt to society.

Your whole future is before you. What are you doing about it?

16

SIXTEENTH DAY

HOPE

Our Lord one day asked the people what they thought of this case: "A man had two sons; and he came to the first and said: 'Son, go and work today in my vineyard.' But he answered and said: 'I will not,' but afterwards he regretted it and went. And he came to the other and spoke in the same manner. And this one answered, 'I will go, sir'; but he did not go. Which of the two did the father's will? They said: 'The first.' Jesus said to them, 'Amen I say to you, the publicans and harlots are entering the kingdom of God before you' " (Mt 21:28-31).

This parable of our Lord is very seldom quoted. It should be of great consolation to the alcoholic to know that he is comparable to the son who said, by his way of living, that he would not serve but then regretting his action, he began a life of service to his father.

Hope is the virtue by which we firmly trust that almighty God will give us eternal salvation and the means to attain it. A dissolute life, firmly repented, is no obstacle to eternal happiness. In the world, a man's past is unfortunately held against him. Consider the parolee from prison. With almighty God, nothing firmly repented is held against him. What a basis of hope!

Firmly repented. That is why we keep harping on the necessity of steps four through twelve. To fulfill the first three steps is marvelous. A sincere bouquet of orchids to you. Firm repentance requires that we do something about making amends for the faults of the past with a resolution to serve our God the best we can.

There are two vices associated with hope. Too much hope is presumption. Too little, or no hope, is despair. Hope is the middle of the road where traveling is safe. Presumption and despair are the shoulders where we are apt to encounter trouble.

Presumption is that fault where we trust in God and then forget to do anything about it. That was the man in the parable quoted above. He said that he would be faithful and then promptly forgot all about it.

Despair is that fault where we have no trust in God's mercy. If one is a bum, he will always be a bum. One can't make a silk purse out of a sow's ear. So we say. Not much room here for the mercy of God who desires not the death of a sinner but that he be converted and live.

There are pillars of the Church who can be guilty of presumption. Faithful are they to all required attendance at church, but lacking woefully are they in the virtues that really count — charity and justice and kindness and consideration. What a shock on Judgment Day it will be for some who paraded as pillars of the Church when the sober bums walk right past them!

One may be faithful to meetings but to be faithful to the program, he must follow steps four to twelve. Otherwise he is not repentant enough to make restitution, not humble enough to talk to someone about his past faults.

There were two sons. One made good and the other failed. How about you?

CONCERN

"Judged by ordinary standards, the life of Francis Thompson, the nineteenth-century English poet, was a miserable failure. He failed successively as a student, a book agent, a shoemaker's apprentice, and a soldier. At twenty-one he was a drug addict, prematurely aged, sleeping on a park bench, and writing poems on wrapping paper, making his living by running errands and selling matches. Then he was discovered by an editor, Wilfrid Meynell, and his wife, Alice, herself a poet. Thompson went to live with them and stayed with them for years until he died. He devoted himself wholeheartedly to his writings, and his talent was recognized. Of his works, one, his great religious poem — *The Hound of Heaven* — won a place for itself among the most celebrated minor poems in our language. Success is something we must find in our own way by cooperating with God. Poverty and hunger and neglect do not necessarily mean failure, though they are often mistaken for it. We fail only when we give ourselves up for lost, refusing the helping hand of others, persisting in despair" *(Three Minutes A Day – Keller).*

This true story is so powerful a lesson of the dignity of the human being and the importance of seeking out lost souls that it would be a shame to mess it up by process of analysis. But we will try.

Francis Thompson was a drug addict. He was down-and-out like many an alcoholic, reduced to sleeping on park benches. His genius was recognized by an editor. The bum on skid row shows no promise whatsoever, but the recovered alcoholic sees in him a dignity that can be reclaimed by the grace of God. The AA member sees further: Save for the grace of God, he would be living in dark hallways, and somebody else would be giving handouts to him.

The Meynells took Francis Thompson into their home. It would take a very hardy member of AA to take some of these people into his home, but it wouldn't be surprising if it is being done. The charity of AA is so tremendous that all unbelievable acts become believable. At least, if we can't take a "down-and-outer" into our homes, we can take him into our hearts. If we can recognize hidden possibilities in the reject of society and if we can have a warm feeling in our hearts in understanding his wretchedness, then we have the heart of charity which far exceeds any amount of almsgiving which is properly named fountain-pen philanthropy.

The twelfth step of AA is a God-given principle. If the alcoholic has found success through the grace of God, then he must never look upon anyone as a failure. Granted that a man may be helpless and may always remain helpless, but in our thinking we must strive never to use the word hopeless. Helpless, YES. Hopeless, NO.

The alcoholic must help himself. We can beat our brains out at times trying to help him and get nowhere fast. There is only so much we can do and then we can leave him to himself. But, if a vulture will hover over a wounded animal until he dies, so the twelfth-stepper can hover over the helpless, but not hopeless, as long as necessary. Words may fail, scoldings may be resented, and kindness ignored, but prayer is always helpful. The sponsor may be licked, but in gratitude he never gives up and keeps praying that by the grace of God success will replace failure.

GOD'S PURSUIT

"I fled Him, down the nights and down the days;
  I fled Him, down the arches of the years;
I fled Him, down the labyrinthine ways
  Of my own mind; and in the midst of tears
I hid from Him, and under running laughter.
  Up vistaed hopes I sped;
  And shot, precipitated,
Adown Titanic glooms of chasmed fears,
  From these strong Feet that followed, followed after."

These are the opening words of *The Hound of Heaven* by Francis Thompson. In this poem he identifies almighty God as the Hound of heaven who relentlessly pursues his prey who is running away from the grace of God. Remember that Francis was a down-and-outer and was at the end of his rope when he achieved sanity. Thompson has projected his thinking into the lines of this poem.

"In the midst of tears He hid from Him." No one knows the remorse of the alcoholic but the alcoholic himself or those in his fellowship. The tears that have been shed; the remorse that has been felt; yet the tears flow so copiously that they fog the eyes which cannot perceive God's nearness.

"I hid from Him under running laughter." Alcohol gives a glow. It peps up the spirits. It produces laughter, sometimes hollow, sometimes boisterous, but as many a clown has been sad, very sad, beneath his laughter, so also is the alcoholic who appears to be bright and gay to the world. His laughter is only a cover-up to blanket out the grace of God which seeks to reclaim him to sobriety and thence to peace and happiness.

"Yet, was I sore adread, lest, having Him, I must have naught besides." Francis Thompson could hear the insistent beat of the feet of the Hound of heaven seeking him out, yet he was afraid to give up what he had, the comfort and euphoria of his drugs. The Higher Power sought him out, but he kept running away and the Hound of heaven kept up his unhurried chase.

To commit self to a Higher Power — what have you really given up? Don't let remembrance of the happy days fool you — even they were a cover-up for the deep-down hollowness and sense of worthlessness. To have the Higher Power and sobriety is to have everything. It is enough.

"Across the margent of the world I fled." How this fits so neatly into the picture of alcoholism. The geographical cure is running away from a problem and hoping to find the answer in a different locality. Thompson would have settled for any answer except the one that would help him and that is why he kept running away from God.

Thompson protested that the infinite Designer was charring the wood before he could draw with it. A dissolute life is a charred life, but a life of sobriety draws a beautiful picture before God and men.

The Hound of heaven tells Thompson that all that was taken from him was safe in the arms of the Higher Power. "Rise, clasp my hand, and come!"

Finally, Thompson allows the Hound of heaven to catch up with him. He then realizes that his gloom and sadness and misery were but the shadow of the hand of God outstretched to bless him.

This poem is a bit heavy, but you may procure a copy from your library; you will get a clear-cut picture of the alcoholic running away from the Hound of heaven, his Higher Power, who pursues him relentlessly for the purpose of bringing him sobriety.

LOYALTY

The Chinese say that one picture is worth a thousand words. This is the picture that appeared on one of the calendars put out by the late Father Flanagan of Boys Town, Nebraska. It is the picture of the home for homeless boys. It is snowing. A fourteen-year-old boy is walking up the pathway that leads to the warmth of the home. In his arms, he is carrying a nine-year-old boy. Evidently, they both started to go together to Boys Town, and the younger boy grew weary in walking. In order to reach his destination, the older boy had to carry the one who was unable to walk. The caption is terrific: "He ain't heavy, Father, he's my brother."

Christian art, which is found in the catacombs of Rome, shows two scenes of Christ, the Good Shepherd. The first depicts the Good Shepherd watching over the sheep in the fold. The second shows the Good Shepherd leaving the ninety-nine in the fold and going out to seek the one that was lost. He finds the lost sheep, places it on his shoulder, and returns to the safety of the sheepfold. Watching over sheep is seemingly effortless. Carrying a lost sheep home may be a bit backbreaking.

Twelfth-step work may entail a lot of backbreaking effort. The long hours spent in seeking out the newcomer who has flown, the abuse that one has to take, the weariness of listening to maudlin mumblings, and the thanklessness of it all, at times. When you grow weary, when the burdens seem insupportable, then remember, "He ain't heavy, Father, he's my brother."

The work that Dr. Albert Schweitzer did in Africa was backbreaking. The work that Dr. Tom Dooley did in Laos was burdensome. The work that the young members of the Peace Corps have done was not easy. They did it for their brothers.

One of the medical corpsmen who worked with Doc Dooley said:

"He does things for people who ain't got it so good." Tough as it may be for us, the ones we work for really have a hard time also. They ain't got it so good. The poor man who is living with a monkey on his back doesn't realize the pitiful condition of his life. It is hard for him to figure that the euphoria he experiences is only compounding his troubles and his headaches. There was one AA member who always told himself in time of trouble, "There is no trouble of mine that booze will cure." If a man ain't got it so good, he may hit the bottle and frequent the gin mill; but when he wakes up the next morning he still ain't got it so good — his mouth will feel like the bottom of a bird cage.

No matter how low a man may have sunk, no matter how miserably he acts — he is still our brother. The twelfth-stepper is the good shepherd who is willing to carry his brother on his back to the sanity he has lost through sickness.

20

CONVICTION

In the Old Testament Book of Nehemiah, the author mentions the fact that while rebuilding the wall around the city of Jerusalem, his enemies resented his work. Yet Nehemiah kept faithfully to his task. There were those at the foot of the wall who scoffed at him. They looked upon the job as a hopeless one. To the taunts of the onlookers, Nehemiah replied, "I am doing a great work, and I cannot come down" (Neh 6:3).

The men in AA are doing a great work. There are those who do not understand the grace of God in the work, do not understand the debt of gratitude that sobriety must return, and do not understand that this great work can be accomplished in AA.

He is a "hopeless" alcoholic. He is too far gone. He is completely helpless. There are thousands upon thousands of alcoholics who have hit the bottom and are sober today because a fellow-man would not be discouraged in twelfth-step work. Suppose thirty twelfth-step calls are made on the same newcomer and then discouragement sets in and the work is discontinued. But suppose further that under God the thirty-first call would have done the trick?

In the AA files, there must be some revealing cases of the return of the "hopeless" and the helpless. In insurance, a man is written off if he is a poor risk. This work is not insurance. This is brotherhood. Real brotherhood is where charity abounds, and faith is the motivating force. The same faith that shows up in the second step is the faith that is breathed into the helpless in twelfth-step work.

Great work is being done in twelfth-step activity. The scoffers would suggest quitting. The discouraged will not believe that anyone can help. Nehemiah had an idea and would not be talked down. The twelfth-stepper has a conviction, a personal conviction, that his program will work; and he will continue despite the hopelessness of the odds.

The race tracks are a very popular place of entertainment where a man can place a legal wager on the outcome of a given race. The parimutuel boards give the odds on the race. The favorite claims the attention of most of the fans. These are the chalk players. The longshot has only an outside chance of winning. His supporters are not numerous, but they are loyal. The payoff on a longshot is the greatest.

So it is with human nature. The mob will bet on the favorite. It is seemingly hopeless to bet on the longshot. The AA believes that there is a chance for the longshot. By the fact that a horse is in the race, he has a chance of winning. Of course, for some "dogs," all the others may have to drop dead. In the human race, a man under God has a chance of rehabilitation even though the odds are stacked against him.

'Tis a great work you are doing. Please don't give it up. Don't let discouragement, ingratitude, fatigue, con men, sharpies, and the maudlin mumblers discourage you.

OBLIGATION

No one can forget this scene from the Bible: "And the Lord said: 'Simon, Simon! Satan, you must know, has got his wish to sift you all like wheat; but I have prayed for you, Simon, that your faith may not fail, and once you have recovered, you in your turn must strengthen your brother.' 'Lord,' he answered, 'I would be ready to go to prison with you, and to death.' Jesus replied, 'I tell you, Peter, by the time the cock crows today you will have denied three times that you know me' " (Lk 22:31-34).

Peter was a great man. We recommend him as the patron saint of the alcoholic. The Semites were very little prone to the disease. But Peter was so human. He always opened his big mouth at the wrong time and always seemed to say the wrong thing. Yet, our Lord saw through the human faults to the greatness that was Peter's and made him the head of the apostles. Would that we could always see through the frailties of the sodden sot and discover the greatness that can be there under God.

Why did our Lord allow Satan to sift Peter like wheat? Frankly, we do not know. Why are some alcoholic, others diabetic, others tubercular, others cancerous, and others free from all disease? We do not know. This *why* is the most provocative three-letter word in the English language. This we can learn from the human weakness of Peter. Our Lord said: "But I have prayed for you, Simon, that your faith may not fail, and once you have recovered, you in your turn must strengthen your brother." This should be a consolation to the alcoholic. The Lord knows of his problem. The Lord is with him in his trials and troubles. When the slip and the bounce threaten, please realize that you are not alone, that the Lord is with you. That is why it is important to pray and meditate by command of the eleventh step — if for nothing more than to remind the good Lord that he has promised to be with you.

The slip and the bounce can be worse than the original fall into alcoholism. Faith in the second step is again needed. If the Lord is with us, why can't we make good?

Peter's betrayal and his tears of repentance had the shock effect of making him the greatest. "Lord, in spite of my weakness you chose me. Now it's my turn again. I will be with you all the way. It's a two way street."

"And once you have recovered, you in your turn must strengthen your brothers." This is the twelfth step in the words of our Lord. Christ says specifically that you are equipped and appointed to help others. As he sent his apostles into the world to preach the Gospel, he is sending you out on twelfth-step work. That is your commission under God.

Abraham Lincoln, with inspired foresight, said the same thing in 1842: "Those who have suffered by intemperance personally, and have reformed, are the most powerful and efficient instruments to push the reformation to ultimate success." Again: "So with men. If you would win a man to your cause, first convince him that you are his sincere friend."

Why the alcoholic? We do not know. But this we do know — that our Lord has promised to help the alcoholic, and he wishes and commands the sober alcoholic to help his still suffering brother through the fellowship of AA.

PREPAREDNESS

Peter will never forget the time he tried to walk on water: ". . . When evening came, Jesus was there alone, while the boat, by now far out on the lake, was battling with a heavy sea, for there was a head-wind. In the fourth watch of the night he went towards them, walking on the lake, and when the disciples saw him walking on the lake they were terrified. 'It is a ghost,' they said, and cried out in fear. But at once Jesus called out to them, saying, 'Courage! It is I! Do not be afraid.' It was Peter who answered. 'Lord, he said, 'if it is you, tell me to come to you across the water.' 'Come,' said Jesus. Then Peter got out of the boat and started walking towards Jesus across the water, but as soon as he felt the force of the wind, he took fright and began to sink. 'Lord! Save me!' he cried. Jesus put out his hand at once and held him. 'Man of little faith,' he said, 'why did you doubt!' And as they got into the boat the wind dropped. The men in the boat bowed down before him and said, 'Truly, you are the Son of God' '' (Mt 14:23-33).

This is our patron saint, Peter. He really was putting on an act. And he actually did walk a few feet. Then he must have asked himself what he was doing walking on the water. As long as he had faith in our Lord, he could do so. When he tried to do it with human reasoning, he began to sink. Yet, our Lord was there all the time and stretched out his hand and supported Peter. But Peter was smart, for he knew where to turn when he was in trouble.

There was a storm at sea. The life of the drinker is definitely a whipped-up storm of great fury. Hurricanes and tornadoes are common in the stormy life of a drinker. We are at the mercy of the storms that buffet the land and the sea, but the storms brought by drinking can be controlled a great deal through the AA program.

When a hurricane approaches the Florida coast, sand bags are erected against the fury of the storm before it hits. When one has sobriety, storms may still approach; but they do give a warning. The best barrier that can be erected is the eleventh step. Of course, it is also understood that help is as near as the telephone or the first AA meeting. The eleventh step takes nothing away from AA. It is AA. It is sandbagging sobriety.

Peter was smart. Oh, so smart! When he began to sink, he knew what to do. He cried out, "Lord, save me!" That is why we recommend that Peter be the patron saint of alcoholics. Humanly, he gets himself into trouble. Supernaturally, he knows how to get out of trouble. The formula is simple. Just cry out to the Lord to save you. That one act is humility. Besides crying out, Peter took the proffered hand of our Lord. Don't expect the Lord to help you during the storm unless you are prepared in humility to do something about accepting the hand of the Higher Power.

"O thou of little faith, why didst thou doubt?" There is that second step again. How often, in the Gospels, does our Lord ask and demand that faith be given before he extended a helping hand.

You know, the twelve steps and the teachings of our Lord are not too far apart.

23

TWENTY-THIRD DAY

HUMAN FRAILTY

Here is another story about our patron Peter: "They seized Jesus then and led him away, and they took him to the high priest's house. Peter followed at a distance. They had lit a fire in the middle of the courtyard and Peter sat down among them, and as he was sitting there by the blaze a servant-girl saw him, peered at him, and said,

'This person was with him too.' But he denied it. 'Woman,' he said, 'I do not know him.' Shortly afterwards someone else saw him and said, 'You are another of them.' But Peter replied, 'I am not, my friend.' About an hour later another man insisted, saying, 'This fellow was certainly with him. Why, he is a Galilean.' 'My friend,' said Peter, 'I do not know what you are talking about.' At that instant, while he was still speaking, the cock crew, and the Lord turned and looked straight at Peter, and Peter remembered what the Lord had said to him, 'Before the cock crows today, you will have disowned me three times.' And he went outside and wept bitterly'' (Lk 22:54-62).

This is the fearless Peter. This is the man who said that he would sooner go to prison before he would betray the Lord. This is the man who was so proud that he did not want the Master to wash his feet. Yet, there was greatness, a greatness that only our Lord recognized. It was akin to humility because he could admit his weakness and fault and endeavor to do something about it.

The alcoholic is human. He thinks that he is great. He has pride to burn. He is just as good as any other man. He is so engrossed with himself that he hardly listens when people tell him that he is headed for trouble. Yet, the alcoholic is really great. He is great with the greatness that has been bestowed upon him by a Higher Power. The Almighty can see this greatness through the fog of his many faults. Yet, there are a few others who can see greatness in him. The sober alcoholic should be exceedingly grateful to the Lord not only for his sobriety but for his twelfth-step work through which he can see the greatness that is inherent in man.

"And Peter went out and wept bitterly.'' This is one of the tests of greatness — a humility which is strong enough to admit that one can be wrong. Peter was always getting into trouble, but his greatness allied to humility engendered self-revelation of his wrong and the firm decision to do something about it.

A Christian legend, which may or may not be true, says that Peter, in Rome, would arise each morning at the crow of the cock and weep bitter tears. The abundant tears were said to have worn furrows in his face. Were they old age wrinkles? When it came his turn to die, he asked to be crucified head down because he was not worthy to die in an upright position like his Master. Notice how humility appears in the life of Peter. His humility was strong enough to overcome each and every fault. What an inspiration to the alcoholic! No wonder we like Peter.

In following the twelve steps, it is not necessary to weep bitter tears. Tears are sometimes called crocodile. Some there are who can cry at the drop of a hat. Noticeable sorrow is not necessary. A sorrow of the heart and mind, which will repent the faults of the past, is a good sorrow. This sorrow allows no room for resentment and bitterness.

24

HIDDEN GREATNESS

"After the meal Jesus said to Simon Peter, 'Simon son of John, do you love me more than these others do?' He answered, 'Yes Lord, you know I love you.' Jesus said to him, 'Feed my lambs.' A second time he said to him, 'Simon son of John, do you love me?' He replied, 'Yes, Lord, you know I love you.' Jesus said to him, 'Look after my sheep.' Then he said to him a third time, 'Simon son of John, do you love me?' Peter was upset that he asked him the third time, 'Do you love me?' and said, 'Lord, you know everything; you know I love you.' Jesus said to him, 'Feed my sheep' " (Jn 21:15-17).

In the courtyard outside the house of the high priest, three times Peter had denied he knew our Lord. This is the human Peter who had boasted that he was willing to go to prison before he would deny the Lord. Our Lord exacted a triple proclamation of love to overcome the triple denial. What was the penance that our Lord gave to Peter for his triple denial? It was the simple avowal, "I love you," repeated three times.

Preceding the above account in the Gospel story, we again see the human Peter at his best. It was after the Resurrection of our Lord from the dead. Simon Peter, Thomas, and four other disciples were fishing in the boat and were not having any luck. Our Lord appeared on the shore and spoke to them. He showed his interest in them, and likewise in us, when he told them where to drop the nets to catch fish. One of the apostles recognized the voice coming from the shore as that of Jesus. The rest rowed to the shore. Not our Peter. He had to jump into the water and swim ahead of the boat.

When they reached the shore, they saw a fire ready, and a fish laid upon it, and bread at hand. What consideration the Lord had for the apostles! What consideration and love he has for us, and in a special way for the alcoholic. Jesus Christ, the risen Lord, the Son of the almighty God, cooking fish on a fire for his friends. You, the alcoholic, are a friend of the Lord. That is why you bother to pray and meditate through the eleventh step. The Lord cares for you — so you must care for each other.

Why did Jesus command Peter to feed the lambs and sheep? He was not a shepherd except in the parables he used. Our Lord simply wants us to take care of our fellow-man.

The two great commandments are the love of God and the love of neighbor. If we believe that a Higher Power has restored us to sanity, then why should we not love him with all our heart, all our mind, and all our strength. And we should love our neighbor as ourselves. If the Lord commands this and commissions us to care for our fellow-man, then the twelfth step makes a great deal of sense.

Peter is outstanding in his closeness to us. He is so much like ourselves. It is not necessary that we imitate his faults and failings. That would be too easy. We should imitate his greatness. This is done precisely through steps eleven and twelve of the AA program.

REMORSE

"Then one of the Twelve, the man called Judas Iscariot, went to the chief priests and said, 'What are you prepared to give me if I hand him over to you?' They paid him thirty silver pieces, and from that moment he looked for an opportunity to betray him" (Mt 26:14-16).

"When he found that Jesus had been condemned, Judas his betrayer was filled with remorse and took the thirty silver pieces back to the chief priests and elders. 'I have sinned'; he said 'I have betrayed innocent blood.' 'What is that to us?' they replied. 'That is your concern.' And flinging down the silver pieces in the sanctuary he made off, and went and hanged himself" (Mt 27:3-5).

Now, don't get on your high horse. No one is calling the alcoholic a Judas. He is anything but one. He sometimes may have acted like the Judas-goat leading others into intemperance and drunkenness by his bad example; but in relationship to the Master, he is more of a friend that a traitor.

There is herein a very important lesson. It is the lesson of hope. It is the lesson of trust. The Lord desires not the death of the sinner but that he be converted and saved. The faith that we learn in the second step teaches us that God is with us and wishes us to be pleasing to him. He does not send us down the road and to the point of no return.

Judas was ashamed. In his shame he came to the high priests who probably laughed at him for his stupidity. That was his mistake. He should have turned to the Lord, and from him he would have found forgiveness. The Gospel verifies this. In the very act of betrayal, Jesus referred to Judas as "friend." This seems to be an open invitation to return to grace.

If the alcoholic meditates on the tragic end of Judas, he can easily realize that there is no room for despair. Judas had separated himself from the thinking of the Master. He had turned his back on him. Yet, the Master had the door open for him, and he pointed to it when he called Judas "friend."

People are right when they say that a man may be down, but he is never out. Judas was down, and he was "out" only because he turned the wrong way. The alcoholic responds to grace when, in the second step, he comes to believe that a Higher Power can restore a man to his sanity.

Peter and Judas. Two human beings with human faults. One was humble and turned to God; the other despaired and turned his back on God. He did not accept the invitation of a Friend who regarded him as a friend. No alcoholic need ever despair when there is hope present.

SOUL SEARCHING

"And so the kingdom of heaven may be compared to a king who decided to settle his accounts with his servants. When the reckoning began, they brought him a man who owed ten thousand talents; but he had no means of paying, so his master gave orders that he should be sold, together with his wife and children and all his possessions, to meet the debt. At this, the servant threw himself down at his master's feet. 'Give me time,' he said, 'and I will pay the whole sum.' And the servant's master felt so sorry for him that he let him go and cancelled the debt. Now as this servant went out, he happened to meet a fellow servant who owed him one hundred denarii; and he seized him by the throat and began to throttle him. 'Pay what you owe me' he said. His fellow servant fell at his feet and implored him saying, 'Give me time and I will pay you.' But the other would not agree; on the contrary, he had him thrown into prison till he should pay the debt. His fellow servants were deeply distressed when they saw what had happened, and they went to their master and reported the whole affair to him. Then the master sent for him. 'You wicked servant,' he said. 'I cancelled all that debt of yours when you appealed to me. Were you not bound, then to have pity on your fellow servant just as I had pity on you?' And in his anger the master handed him over to the torturers till he should pay all his debt. And that is how my heavenly Father will deal with you unless you each forgive your brother from your heart" (Mt 18:23-35).

This parable does not need much explanation. It teaches a lesson. Unfortunately, many, upon reading it, do not understand that they should apply it to themselves. In meditation, we think over the subject matter and then ask ourselves if it means anything in our lives.

We have the same message in the Lord's prayer. Forgive us our trespasses as we forgive those who trespass against us. Oh! how forgiving we are when it concerns us! How thoughtless we can be when it concerns somebody else. Consideration of others is the meat of steps eight, nine, ten, and twelve.

We wonder how many twelfth-steppers demand more of others than was demanded of them on the road to respectability. The unmerciful servant is only a picture of ourselves that we can understand only through prayer and meditation.

A big debt was forgiven to us by the Higher Power. A big load was taken off our shoulders. We are most unmerciful if we fail in consideration of others in the twelfth step.

Our sobriety wiped out a big debt. That is a huge amount. Yet, is it true that we are most unforgiving in little matters? Strange as it may seem it is easier to be heroic in a big thing than it is to be merciful and kind in a multitude of lesser things.

Strange twist. A drunkard formerly was cast into prison by society for his fault. Yet our Lord teaches us that it is possible for us to be cast away for failure to overcome smaller faults. How about it in your life?

VICTORY

"They then took charge of Jesus, and carrying his own cross he went out of the city to the place of the skull or, as it was called in Hebrew, Golgotha, where they crucified him with two others, one on either side with Jesus in the middle" (Jn 19:17-18). "After this, Jesus knew that everything had now been completed, and to fulfill the scripture perfectly he said: 'I am thirsty.' A jar full of vinegar stood there, so putting a sponge in the vinegar on a hyssop stick they held it up to his mouth" (Jn 19:28-29). "They gave him wine to drink mixed with gall, which he tasted but refused to drink" (Mt 27:34).

Consider the thirst of Jesus after his cruel scourging, crowning with thorns, way of the Cross, and Cruxifixion. How dry his mouth must have been! In the account of Matthew, it is recorded that he would not drink. What a consolation to the alcoholic! Christ on the Cross was thirsting for the rehabilitation of the alcoholic. The eleventh step leads us to the conviction that Jesus understands the alcoholic and that he will help him to maintain sobriety.

In society there are well-intentioned people who will offer drink to the alcoholic. They simply do not know; neither do they understand. Take away the first drink, or bring a gallon jug! The alcoholic cannot and should not take the first drink. His inspiration is Jesus who would not taste the proferred wine in order not to assuage his burning thirst.

A thirst, for many, is a condition that can be alleviated. A thirst, for the alcoholic, is a definite compulsion, a sickness, which cannot tolerate the first drink. One day at a time. Easy does it. First things first. Please do not test your sobriety by sitting in barrooms even though it can be done. Do not strive for impression at various cocktail parties. It still can be done, but it is not to be recommended.

The thirst of Jesus on the Cross allows for an identification with the alcoholic. It puts you in the best company. Ask yourself why Jesus thirsted on the Cross. It helps your situation in life to become more bearable. With Jesus, you are nailed to the cross; but need it be considered a cross? The Cross of Christ is the greatest victory. The cross of sobriety is a magnificent victory allied to the sacred thirst of Christ on Calvary.

In the redemption of mankind, Jesus thirsted for souls from the Cross. From his cross of sobriety, the alcoholic thirsts for the rehabilitation of others who are afflicted with alcoholism. The twelfth-step work is a positive action for good. It brings with it understanding and compassion. Christ said that he had compassion on the multitude. The man of sobriety has compassion for the alcoholic who knows not that he can be helped, who too often wills not to be helped. Twelfth-step work is the fulfillment of and an ennobling of the thirst of the alcoholic.

These thoughts on the eleventh step have brought a great consolation to the author. It has enabled him to understand the compassion of Christ much more. May it help you to know that you are identifying Christ with the alcoholic, and that the good you do for others consoled Christ as he suffered for these alcoholics on Golgotha.

—————————————————————— **TWENTY-EIGHTH DAY**

RECOGNITION

"Some time after this there was a Jewish festival, and Jesus went up to Jerusalem. Now at the Sheep Pool in Jerusalem there is a building, called Bethzatha in Hebrew, consisting of five porticos; and under these were crowds of sick people — blind, lame, paralysed —

waiting for the water to move; for at intervals the angel of the Lord came down into the pool, and the water was disturbed, and the first person to enter the water after this disturbance was cured of any ailment he suffered from. One man there had an illness which had lasted thirty-eight years, and when Jesus saw him lying there and knew he had been in this condition for a long time, he said, 'Do you want to be well again?' 'Sir,' replied the sick man, 'I have no one to put me into the pool when the water is disturbed: and while I am still on the way, someone else gets there before me.' Jesus said, 'Get up, pick up your sleeping-mat and walk.' The man was cured at once, and he picked up his mat and walked away'' (Jn 5:1-9).

Now there was lying there a multitude of the sick and the blind. How this fits into the pattern of the active alcoholic! These are sick men. We shall continue to regard them as sick men until medical science comes up with a better explanation. They are more than sick; they are also blind — blind to their own sickness. To the observer, they stagger all over the place, but to themselves they are too blind to see that they are in need of help.

This poor infirm man knew that he was crippled. He also waited for a cure. He must have gone to considerable trouble to get himself placed by the pool. He also knew that he had an outside chance of being helped. Until the alcoholic knows he has a problem and cries out for help, he is in no position to be aided. The first step is recognition of the problem.

Near this pool there was lying a great multitude of the sick. Statistics are not always correct; but in 1972 the figure of 10,000,000 alcoholics was used. This may be an underestimation. The number may be greater. The number is growing, day-by-day.

Through the fellowship of AA, nearly 750,000 have been aided. This would be less than ten percent. What a field for the twelfth-stepper to work. It requires a lot of patience, prayer, and perseverance; but the program calls for just that.

One has said that there is an alcoholic devil who beguiles his victim into believing that no problem is present. This devil is the guy who rides the monkey that rides on the alcoholic's back. How consoling it is to know that there is an alcoholic angel (sober of course) who comes at certain times to lead poor people by the hand into the association of AA.

How more consoling it is to know that the same Jesus who cured the crippled man by the pool of Bethzatha is the Higher Power who will restore a man to his sanity through the fellowship of AA. But, and it is a big consideration, one must use the second step which is faith — faith that we are in the hands of the Higher Power who will help us.

29

HUMAN DIGNITY

It was a Friday afternoon in Dallas, Texas. The date was November 22, 1963. Around noon the phone rang in the Holy Trinity Rectory. The crisp voice of the operator said: "Father, an emergency. D.O.A." The priest picked up his holy oils and drove to the emergency entrance of the Parkland Hospital. He noticed the crowd bustling around the entrance and thought to himself that this must be a V.I.P. Inside the doctors were working feverishly over the patient. The voice of the priest: "I absolve you from your sins and censures, in the name of the Father, and of the Son, and of the Holy Spirit." Dipping his thumb into the holy oils, he made, with his thumb, a small sign of the cross on the forehead of the blood-spattered face: "Through this holy anointing and through the mercy of God may there be forgiven you whatever sins you have committed." A second glance at the patient before turning away — it was a V.I.P. It was John Fitzgerald Kennedy. It was the President of the United States. Hidden beneath the blood-spattered appearance was the identity of the number one citizen of our country.

Christ identifies himself with his creatures. "As often as you give a drink of cold water in my name, you give it to me." Whatever we do for the creatures of God, we do for God himself. Histories of the saints record many examples where a holy man has given help and aid to a leper only to find that he had given that help to Christ.

Saint Christopher is the patron saint of automobile drivers. Christopher means "Christ Bearer." It is related that Christopher made it his job to ford streams with passengers on his back. On one occasion his passenger was unbearably heavy, but he performed his task with his usual patience. Then it was revealed to him that he was actually carrying Christ on his back as he forded the stream. Hence the name of Christopher — Christ bearer.

It should be a comfort to the twelfth-stepper to know that what he does for the miserable drunkard, he is really doing for Christ. Beneath the splash of blood was the face of our President. Beneath the grime of the drunkard is the dignity of man — a greatness bestowed by the Higher Power.

Christopher carried a great burden on his back. How great are the burdens encountered in doing twelfth-step work? How many rationalize, become resentful, bitter, stupid and craven? "It isn't the drinkin' that makes 'em stinkin'; it's the stinkin' thinkin' that keeps 'em drinkin'."

Faith and courage are needed to see beyond the filth to the greatness and dignity of man. An army general observed a nun washing the sores of a leper and he said: "I wouldn't do that for a million dollars." The nun kept on with her work and said: "Neither would I." What she wouldn't do for money, she would do for love. She really believed that she was caring for Christ in the leper, and she had the courage of her conviction.

It is not easy to care for the depraved. But if Christ identifies himself with his creatures, then it becomes easier to do what we must because we are doing it for the Lord.

EMPATHY

"When the Son of Man comes in his glory, escorted by all the angels, then he will take his seat on his throne of glory. All the nations will be assembled before him and he will separate men one from another as the shepherd separates sheep from goats. He will place the sheep on his right hand and the goats on his left. Then the King will say to those on his right hand, 'Come, you whom my Father has blessed, take for your heritage the kingdom prepared for you since the foundation of the world. For I was hungry and you gave me food; I was thirsty and you gave me drink; I was a stranger and you made me welcome; naked and you clothed me, sick and you visited me, in prison and you came to see me.' Then the virtuous will say to him in reply, 'Lord, when did we see you a stranger and make you welcome; naked and clothe you; sick or in prison and go to see you?' And the King will answer, 'I tell you solemnly, in so far as you did this to one of the least of these brothers of mine, you did it to me' " (Mt 25:31-40).

Christ identifies himself with his creatures. He identifies himself with those who are in need. He says in most beautiful, plain language that he is in the hungry, the thirsty, and the sick; and as often as we do anything for these people, we are doing it for him. What a boon to twelfth-step work, a promise of the reward of eternal happiness for doing the work of charity.

Thousands of noble young men and women are dedicating themselves to the work of caring for the underprivileged in many benighted countries. Is it a thrill they seek, akin to joining the Navy and seeing the world? Rather, it is a challenge. So much good to be done and so few and so little time to do it! Then, there is the noble principle that their hearts are filled with charity, that they see Christ in the afflicted and the suffering. These lay volunteers have a vocation. You, as an alcoholic, have a vocation that is not given to all men.

These young people accept a real challenge in going to foreign lands and identifying themselves with the poor. There is a real challenge in working for the alcoholic. You really are one with them.

A certain thrill comes from doing something that is really good and constructive. There was a young nurse who volunteered her services for a medical clinic in a foreign land. Her services were tendered free of gratuities, but her reward was in working for the underprivileged. To her surprise, she found that she was able to set up a tuberculosis program that would add years to the lives of her people. While you work with the drunks, you are working for Christ. It takes an act of faith to see Christ in the low-bottom drunkard, but he says that he is there.

The volunteers for foreign service, in the care of the needy, get very little pay as far as dollars are concerned; but how consoling is the realization that one has been helped. The twelfth-stepper gets nothing in return as far as money is concerned, but how great is the reward in satisfaction!

And for those afflicted with or affected by alcoholism:

Alcohol and the Family
by Father Frank, C.SS.R.

Every year, more and more people fall victim to the disease of alcoholism. It's a problem that reaches beyond the individual alcoholic to affect family, friends, and associates. This book offers hope and HELP. It explains why the three organizations that have helped so many — Alcoholics Anonymous, Al-Anon, and Alateen — have been successful. The first organization confronts the problem of the alcoholic; the other two, the problems of the family. The message of this book is that "there is someone who can help." *64 pages, $1.50.*

Also available in a Spanish edition, **El Alcohol y la Familia,** *64 pages, $1.50.*

*Order from your local bookstore
or see the next page.*

Further reading on the subject of alcoholism:

Are You Becoming an Alcoholic?

by Father Frank, C.SS.R.

This very popular self-examination pamphlet answers quite simply the questions: What is alcoholism? What is an alcoholic versus a heavy drinker? What signs indicate alcoholism? It also describes what Alcoholics Anonymous can do for those who have the disease of alcoholism. *24 pages, 35¢.*

Teenage Drinking

by Thomas W. Klewin

Addressed to both teenagers and parents, this pamphlet discusses what alcohol can do to a person, myths about drinking, and how to USE rather than ABUSE alcohol. *24 pages, 35¢.*

To order the books, booklets, and pamphlets described above and on the preceding pages contact your local bookstore or write to:
Liguori Publications, Box 060, Liguori, Missouri 63057
(Please add 50¢* for postage and handling.)
*For single pamphlet order, send 35¢
plus a stamped, self-addressed envelope.